This story initiates a trend in writing to children touching essential life topics while maintaining a simple language and innocent child imagination. Other stories will follow within the same objective but through different contexts. The topics of this story series will be universal for all ages. Still every generation will have a different communicating style. Life starts with a child's mind perception, so the story will assist children to build up communicating approaches for a comprehensible language as an ultimate goal. The child will have the chance to feel, comprehend and evaluate life values through interacting and conflicting events. Thus he should make the most appropriate decisions and build proper attitudes and behaviors. So the hero of this story will communicate nature and life in different perspectives and contexts, trying to shape his behavioral, functional, and human identity. Children worldwide need to communicate and share nature and life, building a new language helping them discover life and live in harmony among themselves.

One day, Adam woke up to light clicks of a bird on his window glass.. and when he looked at him, he found a weak bird, probably exhausted from a lengthy journey.. he did not think of anything except to feed him and treat him from the fatigue of travel.

He offered him food and water, and he petted him a lot. The bird became happy and safe in the company of Adam, and his behavior turned calm, and he began to sing to Adam despite his extreme fatigue. He had to express his gratitude and happiness

In this sense of euphoria and safety with Adam, the bird surrendered to sleep and said to Adam, "Excuse me, my friend." Adam led him to a warm, safe place.

Adam was amazed and wondered why this bird chose his window and why it felt safe with him quickly? So he kept watching it during his sleep, ensuring that the place was warm and that the bird was sleeping in complete comfort without being disturbed by any noise.

Adam noticed the presence of a message wrapped on the bird's leg. His curiosity led him to open the letter to read what was in it, but he preferred to let the bird rest and ask its permission before he would open it, as it might be for someone else.

The bird woke up early in the morning and went to
Adam's bed until he woke him up with a beautiful song.
It said: "wake up, my friend, a beautiful day has begun..
Let's celebrate the sunrise together.. Let's feel together
feel the sun's warmth.. Let's rejoice the life joys.".

Adam woke up with joy and saw the faint rays of the sun reflecting on something around him in a beautiful view and giving him a delicious warmth. He got up from his bed with joy and started his day chanting the bird's song (Let's enjoy the sun's heat together. Let's rejoice the life's joys).

Adam asked the bird, "Where did you come from, and what brought you here?" The bird replied, "I came from a freezing place in the far North. When it gets too cold, we can't live there, so we look for the warmth in the South in search of life."

Adam asked, "Why do you travel thousands of miles in search of warmth?" The bird said, "This is how we learned from our fathers." We repeat this trip every year. We are happy with this lifestyle.

Adam asked the bird about the message he was carrying. The bird replied: "I do not know its content, but a young girl of your age, who is a friend of mine, asked me to give it to the first person I meet in the warm country. And you are that person. So the message is yours."

Adam took the letter but put it aside and said to the bird, before I read the letter, I want to know how long did it take to travel such a great distance??? Month ?? Two months??? Tell me exactly

The bird said: No, I did not need that long. I am flying at a very high speed that may reach more than two hundred kilometers per hour. I covered more than six thousand kilometers in about three days

Adam said to the bird, I did not expect you to fly so fast. You were going more quickly than a car. The bird replied: "I could double the speed, and there are many birds much quicker than me. But I preferred to enjoy the trip and watch the sea, the sky, and the earth."

Adam asked: How could you fly all this time without food. The bird replied: "I was landing on my way near the shores when I saw fish floating on the surface of the water. So I went to them for food to be able to continue flying.".

Then Adam returned to the message and opened it. He began to read its lines with longing and interest. The bird looked at him to understand, as he did not know its content. So, he said to Adam (Tell me, my friend, what is in this message)

 Adam began reading the message (I am a young girl who lives in an icy and dark town most of the year. I am looking for warmth and light, and I hope that I can go to the South like this bird does. Your country must be beautiful, and you enjoy the warmth and light a lot... .....)

Adam was astonished by the content of this message. He believed that the people of the North enjoyed everything in their country. They do not need the South for anything. He felt happy that he possessed a lot of heat that he did not enjoy much before. So he began to think about the beauty and splendor of it.

Adam asked the bird: "When you will return back to your country so that I can give you a response to this message." The bird answered, "You do not need to wait. My friend gave me another message that I hid under my wing and asked me not to give it to you except when you ask to communicate with her.

The bird gave the other message to Adam, who found different contact numbers to quickly communicate with the sender. Adam was happy with that and said: "What a small world.. I was afraid to wait for months to send my message, but you enabled me to communicate quickly.".

Adam rejoiced the presence of a means of rapid communication across the world and actually began to send her, "Dear, I was lucky to receive your message... I am happy to be your friend and invite you to visit my small, warm village."

 The northern girl said (This bird was my friend, and I envy him for his winter flight. I wish I could fly like him until I reach your warm country to enjoy life. Unfortunately, the cold and the long night here deprive us of that. And even deprives us of communication..)

Adam said: "Yes, my friend, I understand you, but we also suffer from the cold in the winter. Your winter may seem harsher to you, but my winter is still harsh to me. I am also looking for warmth, and I hate the cold..

The northern girl said: Does the cold prevail the whole world and does the entire world need warmth?.. Adam replied: "Yes, we all need warmth, and we all escape from the harshness of the cold..but we can reduce the severity of the cold by promoting mutual understanding and sympathy among humans."

The girl said: "Then let us dream of a world where people love each other and stay away from wars and live with each other in peace.."

Then she added: "How can we become one world, while it is divided into warring countries. It is a miserable world divided by borders and conflicts." Adam said, "But migratory birds do not recognize borders and go wherever they like, so why do borders divide us?

The girl said, "This is what we need. A world without borders." Adam said, "We actually live in a world without borders." The girl said: "How and you cannot enter any country without a travel document and a visa allowing your entry."

Adam said, "But our thoughts fly and migrate from one place to another across the world without any visa. Aren't our thoughts the true expression of our life... then we are in one world at the level of ideas.".

The girl said, "Really, we are in one world that we all share! We have to protect it and make it more beautiful and safer for us all. It is our home and our sanctuary. How beautiful our world is!!..What a beautiful globe we live on!!."

Adam asked: "Why do you like to travel. The girl answered: "I want to discover the world in which we live. This is the right of all of us, and I don't want to wait until I'm old to travel and see the world."

Adam said, "I share your interest, and we can start exploring the world from now on". The girl said in amazement: "How can we do while we cannot travel? You are dreaming, Adam."

Adam said: I am not dreaming, and we will begin the journey of discovery right now. Adam was walking down the road and opened the camera phone and kept roaming and said: "Now I take you with me everywhere I go in my village, and you will see everything. Then I will explain to you everything you saw."

The girl accompanied Adam on his trip to his small village and saw him walking around, playing and chatting with his friends. And she said to him: "Thank you, Adam. I really felt that I visited your village and toured it, and I see that you enjoy a lot of the warmth and the bright sun..and you have a lot of fun and cheerfulness."

Adam said: "That's right." We love company and love humor a lot. We also yearn to discover the world, as we are all earthlings. "Tomorrow," the girl said, "I will take you to my town to visit public places. And you will see by yourself how people live this cold winter.

The next day, the girl contacted Adam and opened the phone camera. She accompanied Adam with her in the city's dark streets because of the short winter's day. The city was almost covered with snow, and the children were playing on the snow in their protective clothing.

Adam said, "This is the first time I've seen these lots of snow. It amazed me that your young children are not afraid of snow but rather play and have fun with it. This is an exciting sight...but your streets are almost empty of pedestrians." The girl said: "That's why I envy you for these large gatherings of people."

The girl said: "Can we participate in another activity. Adam replied: "Yes, we can participate in some electronic games to see who of us has stronger or faster skills", and indeed they participated in some games and shared the fun and exchanged ideas.

Adam said: "The day of the departure of the migratory bird is approaching. Do you want anything from my country? The girl said; "I do not want the bird to carry heavy objects. It is enough for him to return safely to his town, and it is enough that he was the reason for our acquaintance with each other. Adam said: "But wait, I will send you just a message with him."

Adam thought to send a surprise to his friend, so he extracted a camera from one of the old mobiles and turned it into a camera that could work for four days and provided it with a charging battery powered by solar energy. Finally, Adam fixed the camera to the top of the bird's leg.

The bird made the return trip, and the fixed camera recorded a whole movie of all its movements, whether it was in the sky, or while it was approaching the sea to fish, or when finally it was landing at the last stop."

The bird arrived in his original town and went to his friend. She searched for the message and found nothing but a small camera. She emptied it and was astonished by what she saw and said to Adam: "Thank you for your surprising message, I understood it. It says, yes, we can discover the world if we cooperate together. And thanks to you to our migratory bird friend who opened our eyes to this beautiful world."

I dedicate this story to my cute grandson Adam who inspired me to go to the end of this story. Adam is the real hero of the story.

Thank you Adam and keep exploring and loving animals and all forms of our Beautiful life

Adam is the oldest of my six grandchildren. He was very close to me since I witnessed the moment of his birth. He is a courageous adventurous boy who like so much all knid of animal and can communicate with them easily without any fears or restrictions. He lives far away from me in different country, different continent and different langauga and different culture but he is always closest to my feelings and my thoughts. He inspired me this series (adventure in nature).

I taught him few things and I learnt from him a lot. Haapy life and achievement Adam, Life is between your hand and the future is yours.

M.Sitohy

www.ingramcontent.com/pod-product-compliance
Lightning Source LLC
Chambersburg PA
CBHW040148240726
48664CB00002B/634